THE FROG

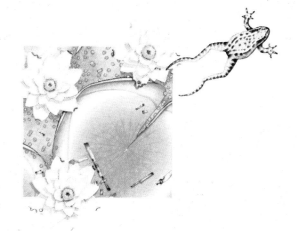

To Tiffany   M.L.

Kivei tinaqu lomani   G.C.

Text copyright © 1981 by Margaret Lane
Pictures copyright © 1981 by Grahame Corbett
All rights reserved.
Library of Congress Catalog Card Number 81-1228
Printed in Italy
First Pied Piper Printing 1982
A Pied Piper Book is a registered trademark of The Dial Press.
First published in Great Britain in 1981 by Methuen/Walker Books

THE FROG is published in a hardcover edition by The Dial Press,
1 Dag Hammarskjold Plaza, New York, New York 10017.
ISBN 0-8037-2748-8

THE FROG

By Margaret Lane

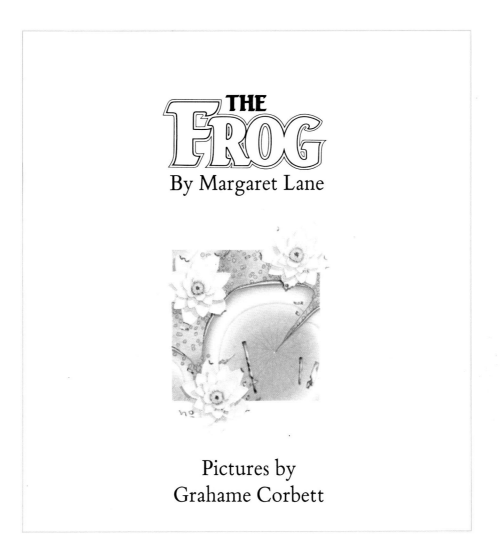

Pictures by
Grahame Corbett

THE DIAL PRESS/New York

If you were born a frog, your first view of the world would be through a film of jelly. Frogs' eggs are laid in ponds, in floating jellylike clusters among waterweeds. The speck in the middle of each egg grows into a tadpole with a little tail and a mouth with horny lips and sharp teeth. Hundreds hatch at the same time and swim around together.

In a few weeks time, if it is not eaten by a hungry fish or diving beetle, each tadpole grows strong hind legs and feet with five toes. Later, smaller front legs appear, with four fingers on each hand. There are webs of skin between the fingers and toes, which help the tadpole to swim fast and to dive under leaves and weeds when it wants to hide. Once all four legs are grown and strong, the tail begins to disappear, and when it is entirely gone, the tadpole has turned into a frog.

This is a great change. Now the tiny frogs can leave the pond, can breathe air, and can live in the mud and grass. They are as much at home on land as they were in water and move by jumping and crawling as well as swimming. Their hind legs become very strong and grow twice as long as their whole bodies. This makes frogs wonderful jumpers. A sudden leap is their best and quickest escape from danger, making them difficult to catch.

The young frogs must now feed themselves in the mud and grass around the pond, and in the weeds that grow in the water. They catch flies, beetles, and butterflies on the end of their long sticky tongues, which lash out like whips. Frogs stuff slugs, worms, and maggots into their mouths with both hands and swallow with a gulp, closing their eyes. They may even eat other tadpoles. But there have always been many creatures eager to eat *them*.

It is not only fish such as pike that are a danger to frogs. Many animals, like rats, otters, and foxes, eat them when they can — and people are no exception. The ancient Romans were especially fond of frogs' legs, and they are still a favorite dish in many parts of the world. They are cooked in sauce, or dipped in batter and fried, and taste a lot like chicken. But luckily for the species, frogs are so difficult to catch that they will never all be eaten.

There are many different kinds of frogs. There are even some with suction disks on their toes and fingers that can jump forty times their own length. But the kind of frog most often seen is the common frog. It lives almost everywhere in the United States and Europe and as far north as the Arctic Circle. It is brownish green with darker spots and yellow eyes.

At a little more than a year old the young frogs are grown-up. They have spent the winter asleep under stones and logs, in damp land or mud, sometimes far from their pond.
In spring the males feel a strong urge to go back there. They often travel a long way, crossing roads and paths and sometimes getting run over by cars. The ones that reach their pond in safety settle down in the mud and shallow water and begin to croak, making a loud noise.

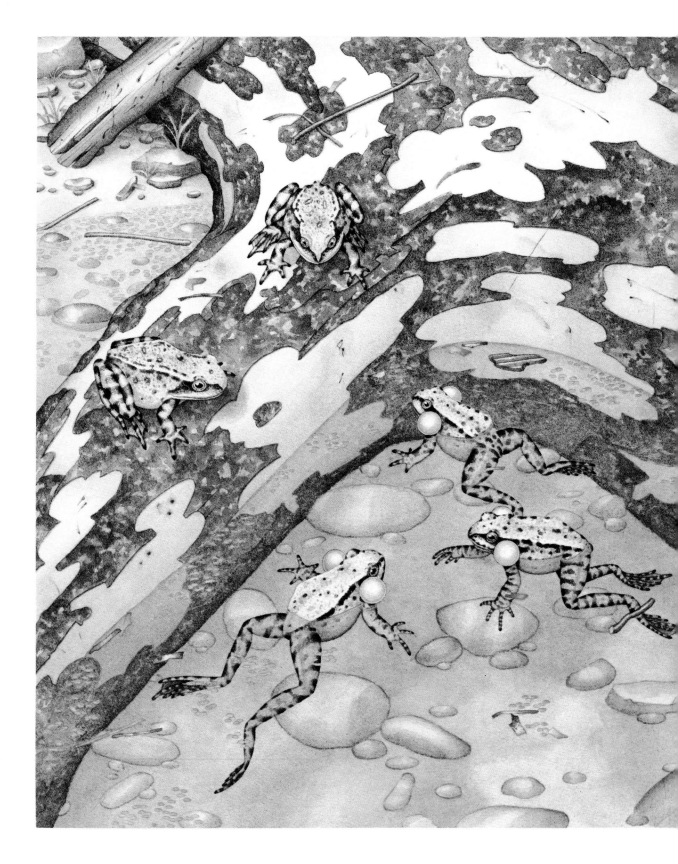

They do this to attract the females
to their pond. It is their love song.
The males have pouches in their cheeks
that fill with air like a balloon
and make a loud sound as they
sit with their heads poking out
from the shallow water. And soon
a few female frogs, bigger than the
males, come slowly through the
grass. They plop into the
water and each chooses one
of the male frogs
as a mate.

While they are mating, the male climbs on the back of the female and clasps her in his arms. She starts to lay her eggs in clumps of jelly, and as these pass over his toes the male sprays them with his sperm, a fluid that starts their development into tadpoles. The jellied eggs, called frog spawn, float away and settle among the weeds. One female lays many thousands of eggs, and when she has finished, she leaves the water and goes off to rest, while the male starts croaking again for another mate.

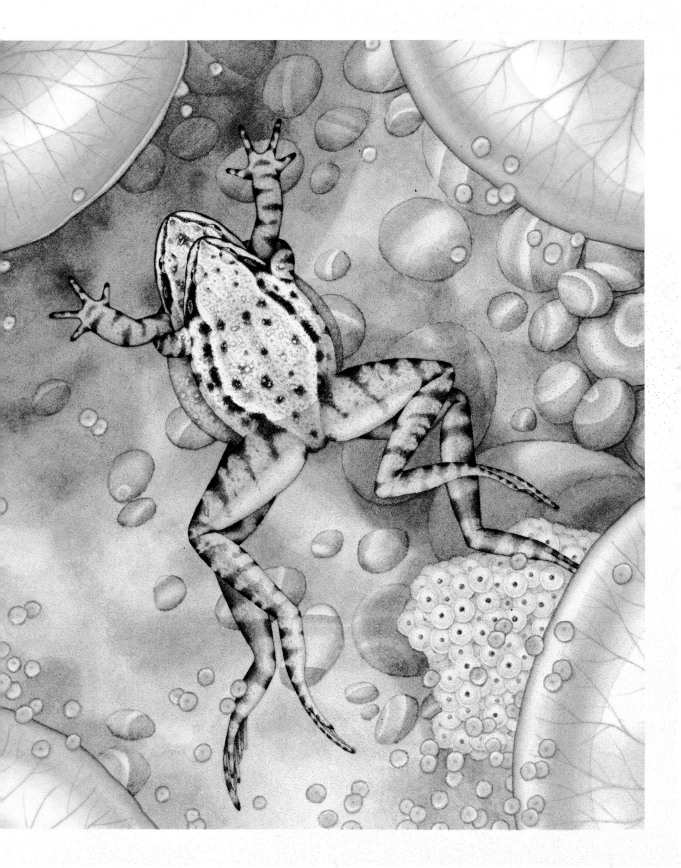

The males stay at the pond until no more females come to answer their call. Then they, too, leave the water and go back to the grass, looking for their next meal. The frog spawn is left clinging to the weeds and lily pads, where most of it will make a meal for birds and fish. In a week to ten days, from the eggs that escape being eaten, a whole new family of tadpoles will wriggle out and begin life on their own.

Life is not as easy for frogs as it used to be. They have always been a prey of other animals and of people. In ancient times it was even thought that witches killed frogs to work magic and weave spells. But today their world is being threatened by the spraying of fields to kill insects, by the draining of ponds, by the building of new roads, and by the cutting of woodlands.

Some people keep frogs as pets. They will live happily only if they have a large glass tank with moist earth, plenty of plants, and a pool of water in it. They must be fed live insects, grubs, and worms, which is not always easy. Frogs are also used by doctors for teaching students. They are kept in cages and then cut up, which is useful to the students but terrible for the frogs. It is a lucky frog today who lives by a quiet pond where it can jump and feed and croak and mate in peace.

About the Author

Margaret Lane is the celebrated author of outstanding books of fiction and biography including *A Night at Sea, A Smell of Burning,* and *The Magic Life of Beatrix Potter.* She has worked as a journalist in London and New York and has written reviews for numerous literary publications.

Ms. Lane was educated at St. Stephen's College in Folkestone, England, and St. Hugh's College, Oxford. She lives with her husband, the 15th Earl of Huntingdon, in Beaulieu, England.

About the Artist

Grahame Corbett was born in Fiji and raised in Fiji, New Guinea, and New Zealand. He studied art in New Zealand and currently lives in London, England. This is his first book.

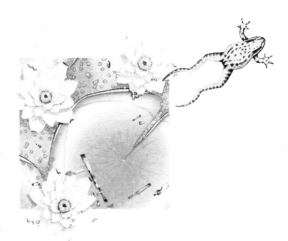

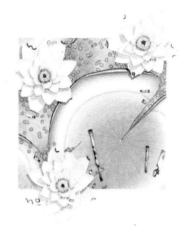